Be a
History
Detective

Tudor Medicine

Dereen Taylor

WAYLAND

This book is a differentiated text version of
The History Detective Investigates Tudor Medicine
by Richard Tames

This edition first published in 2009 by Wayland

Copyright © Wayland 2009

Wayland
Hachette Children's Books
338 Euston Road
London NW1 3BH

Wayland Australia
Level 17/207 Kent Street
Sydney NSW 2000

Editor: Victoria Brooker
Designer: Simon Borrough

British Library Cataloguing in Publication Data:
  Taylor, Dereen
  Tudor medicine. - Differentiated ed. - (Be a
history detective)
  1. Medicine - England - History - 16th century -
Juvenile literature
  I. Title II. Tames, Richard
  610' .9'42'09031

ISN: 978 0 7502 5703 9

Printed and bound in China

Wayland is a division of Hachette Children's
Books, an Hachette UK Company.

www.hachettelivre.co.uk

Picture acknowledgements:
The publishers would like to thank the
following for permission to reproduce their
pictures: The Bridgeman Art Library 15
(Ashmolean Museum, Oxford); 5 (Christie's
Images); 18 (right) (National Portrait
Gallery); 4 (top) (Rafael Valls Gallery,
London); 7 (top and bottom), 9 (left) and
cover, 10, 18 (left), 19, 21, 23 (top), 24 (right),
26, 27 (right); 4 (bottom), 11 (top), 14 (The
Stapleton Collection); The Fotomas Index 20
(right), 22; Hodder Wayland Picture Library
16, 23 (bottom), 27 (left); Mary Evans Picture
Library 1, 6, 8 and cover, 9 (right), 13 (top
and bottom and cover), 20 (left), 24
(bottom); Philip Sauvain Picture Collection
17, 25 (top); Science Museum/Science &
Society Picture Library 12, 28 (top, bottom),
29; The Wellcome Trust 11 (bottom).

Contents

Words in **bold** can be found
in the glossary.

Surviving in Tudor times

Tudor kings and queens ruled England and Wales from 1485 to 1603. At this time, medicine was expensive and very basic. It was hard for Tudors to survive childbirth, violence, accidents and **epidemics**. Death rates were high.

The History Detective, Sherlock Bones, helps you to find clues and collect evidence about Tudor medicine. Wherever you see one of Sherlocks paw-prints, you will find a mystery to solve. The answers are on pages 30 and 31.

Deadly diseases

During the summer, diseases like **smallpox** were common. Many people also died from the **plague**. There were more deaths in towns so many wealthy families moved to the countryside for the summer.

❀ Why do you think it was more dangerous to live in the town than in the countryside?

▶ *Murder was much more common than today. Most Tudor men carried a weapon to protect themselves.*

▼ *The rich Tudors are fleeing to the countryside.*

Childbirth

Childbirth was dangerous. Women could die from blood loss, infection or the baby being in the wrong position. About one in sixteen births killed the mother.

Punishment

Without science to explain sudden death, religion and superstition filled the gap. Christianity taught that death could be god's punishment for wickedness. People also believed **witchcraft** could cause illness or accidents.

This Tudor mother and baby were lucky enough to survive childbirth.

Detective work

Read the list of deaths in your local paper to find out how long people can expect to live in Britain today.

Tudor doctors

The best doctors were called physicians. Physicians were the only doctors who treated illnesses inside the body. They were also able to prescribe medicines to be swallowed. There were less than a thousand physicians in Tudor Britain and their fees were very high.

Surgeons and barbers

Surgeons performed **operations** and treated sores and rashes. Barbers cut hair and also did minor surgery, including pulling teeth. In 1540, the two joined together as the College of Barber-surgeons in London.

Detective work

Visit the websites for the Royal College of Physicians and the Royal College of Surgeons of Edinburgh. Which college is older?

❀ Do you think it is a good or bad idea to use the bodies of **executed** criminals in medicine?

▲ Henry VIII gave barber-surgeons, like those above, the right to cut up the bodies of executed criminals to learn about medicine.

Midwives

Midwives helped women to give birth. They were usually older women with children of their own. They had no training or qualifications.

Travelling doctors

Travelling doctors were quite common. They were called 'mountebanks' or 'quacks'. Some quacks charged people to cure their illnesses and then left before their patients found out they were not real doctors.

Sir Hugh Platt had words of warning for people visiting barbers:

'...all men to be careful how they suffer their teeth to be made white with any Aqua fortis (strong water)... for unless [it] be... carefully applied, a man... may be driven to borrow a rank of teeth to eat his dinner with...'

The Jewel House of Art and Nature (1594)

▲ *Some medicines were sold in special shops.*

✤ What were the dangers of visiting the barber (see panel above left)?

▶ *A Tudor 'quack' doctor performing in front of a crowd.*

How were doctors trained?

Physicians read medical books by ancient Greek and Roman **healers**. The most famous healer was Claudius Galen (AD129–199). He learned about medicine by treating wounded **gladiators**.

The four humours

Galen believed the body was filled with four different 'humours' or fluids. If the body's fluids were unbalanced, it caused illness. A physician restored balance by making the patient sweat, vomit or go to the toilet. He might also make the patient bleed to restore balance.

Detective work

Find out more about the four humours (fluids) that doctors used to think were in the human body.

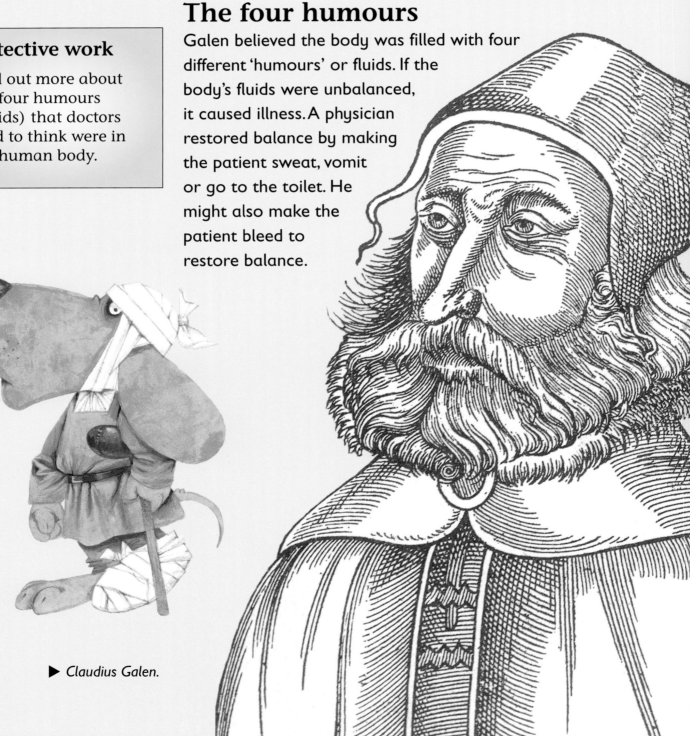

▶ *Claudius Galen.*

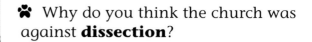

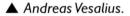

▲ *Andreas Vesalius.*

Why do you think the church was against dissection?

One Tudor doctor said that practising medicine was just as important as reading about it:

'thou shalt never... digest... anything... except... that which thou hast seen before thine eyes and in the practice of thine own hands...'
Dr John Hall (1622)

▼ *Mary, Queen of Scots, gave Scottish barber-surgeons the right to serve as doctors instead of soldiers.*

Dissection

Physicians usually studied at Oxford or Cambridge university. The most senior teachers, such as Andreas Vesalius (1514–64), dissected bodies to find out how they worked. This greatly improved physicians' knowledge of the human body, but the church was against it.

Military doctors

Surgeons often learned how to perform operations by treating soldiers' illnesses and wounds. Many leading doctors trained with military or naval forces.

What wouldn't a Tudor doctor learn if he just treated soldiers?

Making Tudor medicines

Detective work
Search the Internet to find out why modern doctors think spiders' webs might be useful?

✿ Why do you think people used everyday items to make medicines?

Tudor medicines were usually freshly made each time they were needed. They were based on plants or drinks like ale and milk. One doctor used over a hundred different ingredients in his medicines. These included herbs, chicken droppings and spiders' webs.

Tudor medicines

Medicines were used to relieve pain or make people sleep. Some medicines were supposed to restore unbalanced humours (see page 8). Wearing heavy clothes that were

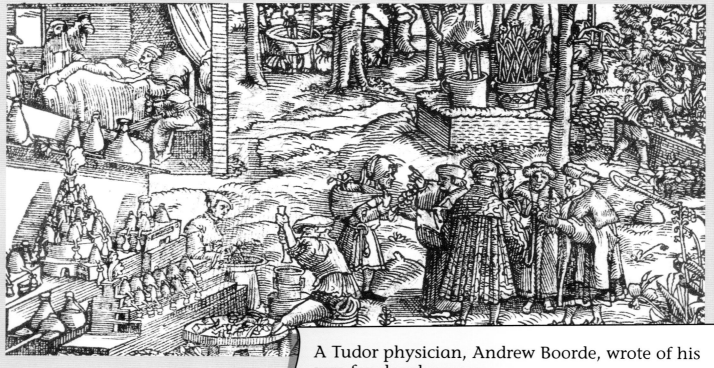

▲ Herbs and plants were grown in this Tudor garden especially to make medicines.

A Tudor physician, Andrew Boorde, wrote of his cure for sleeplessness:

'take of the oil of violets an ounce, of opium half an ounce, incorporate this together with woman's milk and with a fine linen cloth lay it to the temples...'

Breviary of Health (1547)

rarely washed meant people got fleas or **lice**. They needed home-made potions to kill vermin and soothe insect bites.

Herbalists

Many Tudors knew how to use herbs to make medicines. But herbalists were the experts. They knew where to gather each plant and which part of it to use. Tudor herbalists would then turn their ingredients into powders, pills, plasters and ointments.

❧ What problems might there be in using herbs for medicines?

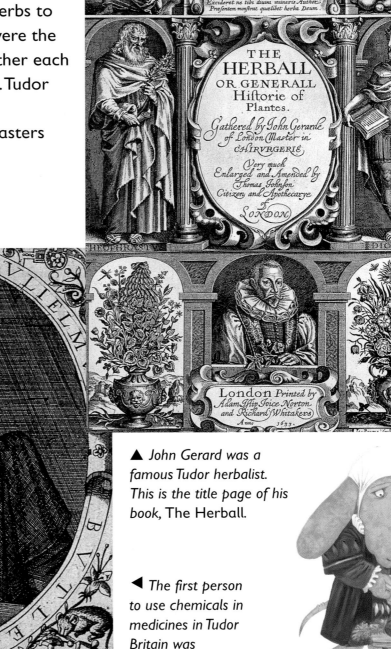

▲ John Gerard was a famous Tudor herbalist. This is the title page of his book, The Herball.

◀ The first person to use chemicals in medicines in Tudor Britain was William Butler.

Tudor operations

Surgery was the very last thing Tudor physicians tried to save a patient. Today, patients are given **anaesthetics** to make them unconscious during an operation. In Tudor times, patients were awake and they often died of pain or shock. Surgeons had to work fast and the best could cut off a leg in under a minute.

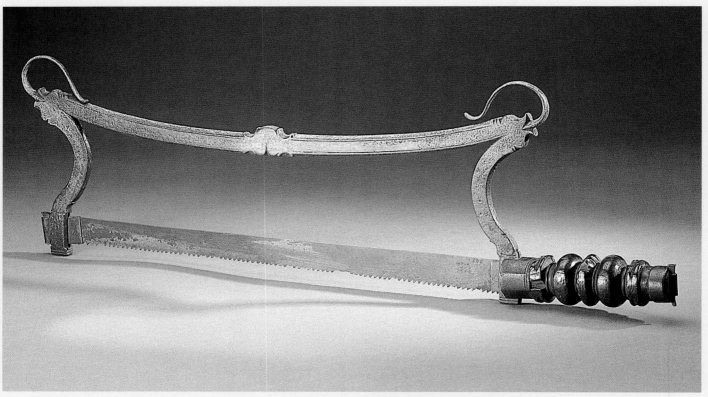

▲ *A good saw was needed to* **amputate** *an arm or leg.*

Battle wounds

Tudor battlefields brought new challenges for surgeons. Gunshots destroyed flesh and muscle. They shattered bone and forced dirty clothing into wounds, causing infection.

Gunshot wounds

John Vigo was an expert on gunshot wounds. He said that wounds should be cleaned with boiling oil, but this often killed the patient.

In 1536, Ambrose Paré (1509–90) was treating soldiers after a battle. He ran out of hot oil and made up a cool dressing instead. He found this worked much better than boiling oil.

◀ *Ambrose Paré.*

Ambrose Paré wrote how hard it was to amputate a limb:

'...who can without pain cut off an arm or leg...? A surgeon must have a strong, stable and fearless hand and a mind determined and merciless...'

✖ What do you think the doctor below would have used to cut off the soldier's leg?

▼ *Paré cuts off a soldier's leg on the battlefield.*

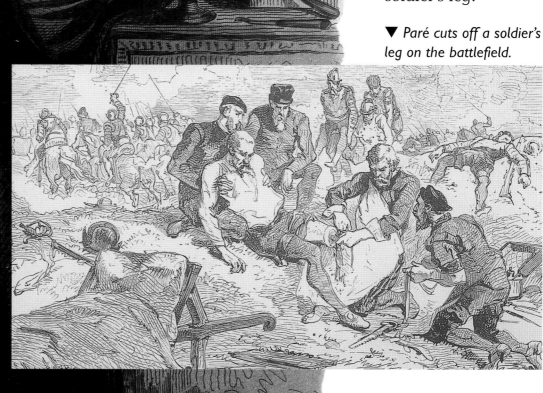

Were there female doctors?

Until the colleges of physicians and barber-surgeons were set up, most people relied on their families to heal them. The teaching of medicine began to need years of study and examinations. As women did not go to school, they found it much more difficult to become doctors.

❖ Do you think the women in the picture below were trained to be midwives?

Female doctors

Girls did not go to school but many noble-women were taught to read and write at home. They could then learn how to make medicines for their family and neighbours.

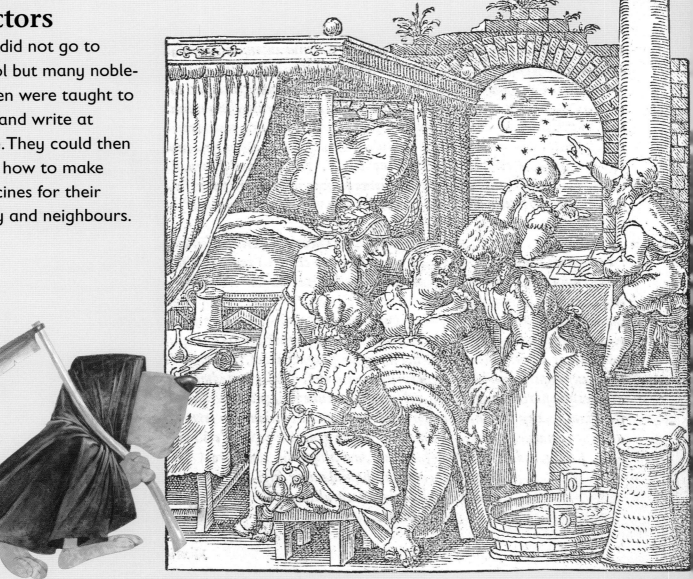

▲ *Most midwives were women.*

▲ *Tudor people thought that a 'white witch' would have a kitchen like this.*

White witches

Many villages had 'wise women' or 'white witches' who made up medicines. Some really were skilled healers but others pretended to be able to use magic to heal people. Witches were often blamed for a sudden sickness or mental illness. This is because people did not have another explanation for illness.

Detective work

Use your local library to find out about people accused of witchcraft in Tudor times. How did people think witches could be identified?

' *...as the killing witch must die, the healing and harmless witch must die... though he kill not... by witches we understand not only those which kill and torment but all diviners, all wizards... commonly called wise men and wise women...*'

William Perkins, *A Discourse of the Damned Art of Witchcraft* (1608)

Were there hospitals?

In 1500, there were hundreds of monasteries and nunneries. The monks and nuns who lived in them cared for the sick. In the 1530s, King Henry VIII closed the monasteries and took away their wealth and land.

▼ *Doctors are making the most of the space available in this hospital ward.*

Tudor hospitals

Later in Tudor times, three important hospitals were set up in London. These were St Thomas's, St Bartholomew's and Bethlehem. Many leading physicians served at these hospitals, including William Harvey (1578–1657) of St Bartholomew's. He made the discovery that blood goes round the human body.

Detective work

St Bartholomew's and St Thomas's hospitals still exist. Use the library and the Internet to find out more about their history.

Lazar-houses

Special hospitals called 'lazar-houses' looked after people with **leprosy**. As leprosy died out, the lazar-houses cared for people with illnesses that could not be cured.

One Tudor physician thought that mentally ill patients should be treated in this harsh way:

'...*every man the which is mad... to be kept... in some... chamber, where there is little light. And that he have a keeper the which [he] do fear... also the chamber... let there be no painted cloths... nor pictures... for such things make them full of fantasies. And use few words to them...*'

Andrew Boorde (1567)

▼ *A lazar-house in Oxford.*

Pest-houses

During epidemics, many towns also set up temporary pest-houses, where the sick went to die. In this way, people hoped to keep infection under control. Some surgeons took patients into their own homes to help them get better.

Who treated royalty?

Royal physicians looked after the health of Tudor royals. It was up to the physicians to make sure that the kings or queens were not poisoned. They also treated illnesses and attended the births of royal children. Royal physicians were very highly paid.

✿ Why do you think that it might have been risky to be a royal physician?

▼ *William Butts was one of Henry VIII's physicians.*

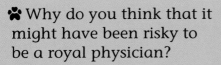

▲ *This painting shows a dying Henry VIII pointing to his son.*

The health of Henry VIII

It is unlikely that Henry VIII's doctors helped his health. The Tudor king suffered from painful **gout** when he was older. By the time he was 50, Henry's legs were so swollen he could hardly walk.

Edward VI

Royal doctors were unable to save Jane Seymour. She died after giving birth to Henry's son, Edward VI. Edward was ill

for much of his short life and died at the age of sixteen.

Queen Mary

Queen Mary, Henry VIII's daughter, was desperate to have a son. When her stomach finally began to grow, she was not having a baby, but suffering from cancer.

◀ *Queen Mary*

✿ Mary's doctor probably knew she was not pregnant, but didn't say anything. Why do you think this was?

'In the very end of May, began in the city of London... the sweating sickness... The king was sore troubled for divers [several] died in the court... so that the King... came to... a place of the Abbot of St Alban's... which place was so purged [cleaned] daily with fires... that... none of their company was infected...'

Edward Hall, *Life of Henry VIII* (1548)

Detective work

Search on the Internet to find out why Roderigo Lopez was hanged and quartered at Tyburn in 1594.

Medical books

Before the invention of printing, books were written by hand and were very expensive. A handwritten bible took three years to copy. A printed book could be made ninety times faster and ten times cheaper. As printing spread through Europe more ordinary people began to be able to read books.

▲ *A fifteenth-century printer's workshop would have looked like this.*

❧ Why do you think newly printed pages were hung up?

▲ *Andrew Boorde, one of Henry VIII's physicians, wrote a book which included cures for baldness and poor eyesight.*

Books

Some doctors wrote reference books for other doctors to use. There were also general books for ordinary people, containing advice about staying healthy. By the time Elizabeth I died in 1603, over 150 medical books had been published in English.

Keeping fit and well

Most health books said that diet, exercise and a healthy environment were all important for good health. Laziness, over-eating and worry were all seen as dangerous. The poor couldn't afford to be lazy or over-eat, so these health books were definitely written for the rich.

▲ *Rich Tudors could play tennis to exercise.*

✿ Why do you think medical writers were only interested in the health of rich, and not poor, Tudors?

In his 1607 poem, Sir John Harrington wrote of the benefits of garlic. Garlic is still seen as a healthy food.

'Since garlic then hath power to save from death;
Bear with it though it make unsavoury breath;'

Medical help for the poor

The poor suffered from illness more than the wealthy. They often ate food that was going bad and lived in crowded rooms. Many got infected or cut at work doing dirty, dangerous jobs.

Detective work

Find out what the poor law was. How did it work in your area?

Caring for the poor

Local government was run by Justices of the Peace (JPs). They split the poor into 'deserving' and 'undeserving'. Undeserving poor were people who were well but refused to work. Deserving poor were unable to work because they were too old or sick. JPs thought deserving poor deserved help because caring for the poor was a religious duty. Also, if deserving poor were cured, they could go back to work.

◀ *Justices of the Peace decided whether the poor deserved help or not.*

▲ *A Tudor beggar is whipped through the streets.*

Thomas Tusser wrote of how a wife could prevent sickness in her husband:

*'Good housewives provide,
Ere a sickness do come,
Of sundry good things in her house to have some...
Good broth and good keeping, do much now and then,
Good diet with wisdom, best comforteth men.'*

The Points of Housewifery United to the Comfort of Husbandrie (1570)

Undeserving poor

A few doctors charged rich patients high fees and then treated the poor for free. People who couldn't be cured might be sent to the lazar-house (see page 17) to be fed and cared for. Undeserving poor lived by begging or stealing. Some JPs thought they should be whipped and **branded**.

✤ Why do you think that beggars were branded?

▶ *A Tudor nobleman ignores a beggar.*

The plague

The black death of 1347–9 was an outbreak of bubonic plague around the world. It was carried aboard sailing ships from Asia to Europe. It was spread by the fleas living on rats.

Plague outbreaks

There were many outbreaks of the plague in London and other cities, before, during and after Tudor times. The plague usually began in the poorest, dirtiest, most crowded areas of a city. The plague struck suddenly and spread rapidly. It was horribly painful and once you had it, you almost always died. Most sufferers had buboes. These were hard, pus-filled boils in the groin and armpits.

Treatments for the plague

When the plague broke out, most physicians ran away to protect themselves. A few doctors stayed to help the sick. Some of their treatments, like burning sores with hot irons, only made the patient worse. Most doctors tending the sick died themselves.

▲ This record shows how many people died in London in just one week.

❧ Can you see how many people died from the plague in the record above?

▼ This painting is called 'Dance of Death'. The artist showed both rich and poor people, because no one could escape the plague.

▼ *This churchyard at Sandhurst in Kent is thought to be where many victims were buried in one huge plague grave.*

Detective work
Find out which nursery rhyme is said to be about the plague.

A city was not the place to be when the plague broke out:

'...all merry meetings are cut off... Playhouses stand... the doors locked up... like houses lately infected, from whence the affrighted dwellers are fled...'

Thomas Dekker (1609)

Learning about the past

Historians find out about Tudor medicine from the records kept by cities and hospitals. The records of the college of physicians or colleges of barber-surgeons show how doctors were trained.

Tudor medical books

Tudor medical books show how doctors spotted illnesses. They also show the treatments they used. These books explain how Tudors thought medicine worked at that time.

Detective work
You can find out about hospital records in your area on the following website: http://hospital records.pro.gov.uk. Which was the first hospital in your area?

▼ *This doctor is treating a patient.*

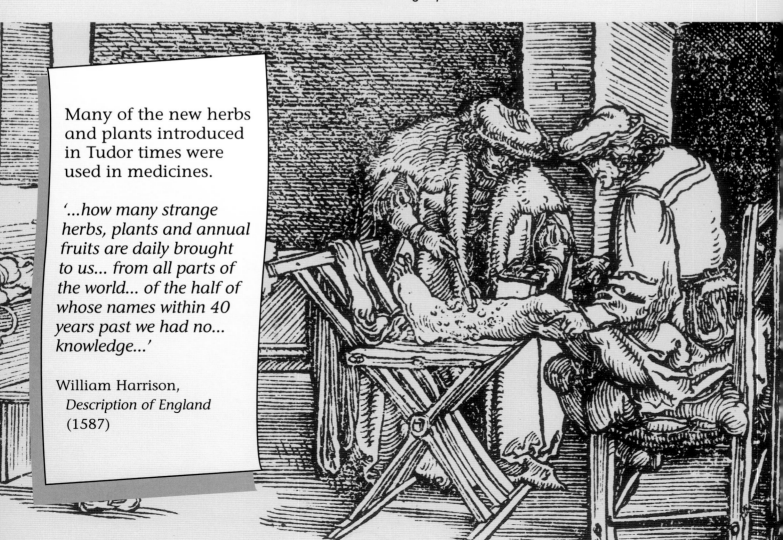

Many of the new herbs and plants introduced in Tudor times were used in medicines.

'...how many strange herbs, plants and annual fruits are daily brought to us... from all parts of the world... of the half of whose names within 40 years past we had no... knowledge...'

William Harrison,
Description of England
(1587)

Illness in families

Letters and diaries tell us that Tudor people worried about illness a lot. Families often kept books of recipes for food, perfumes and medicines all mixed up together.

Teeth and illness

Many Tudors had very good teeth because sugar was too rare to cause tooth decay. Tooth enamel can show if a person suffered from a serious illness. This is useful for historians and archaeologists looking for clues about the past.

▶ *Skeletons can show signs of death from violence, surgical operations or poor diet.*

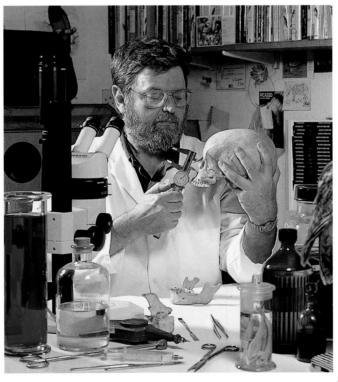

▲ *A museum expert checks a human skull for signs of disease.*

Your project

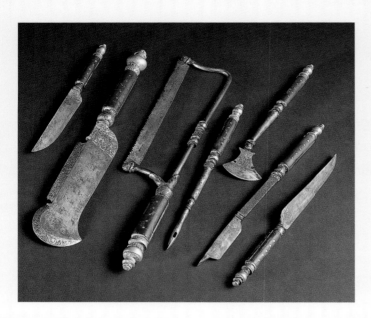

Now you have followed the detective activities in this book, you can track down clues to do your own Tudor medicine project. Choose a topic that you find really interesting – or really gruesome! You could get ideas by looking through this book's index. You could also use one of the questions on page 29 to start you off.

Sixteenth-century surgical instruments.

Topic questions

- What do we know about illness and treatments in Tudor times?
- Can you describe a visit to a hospital in Tudor times?
- If you could interview a Tudor doctor what would you ask?
- Do people still use herbs to treat illness?

Project presentation

- Write an advertisement for a new medicine book for English families in 1600. Include a list of contents and a note about the author and his qualifications for writing the book.
- Put together your own Tudor medicine chest (e.g. rosemary, garlic, honey). Write a book of instructions on how to use them.
- Pretend you are a doctor and write a diary of an outbreak of plague in your town.

In Tudor times, there were special doctors for horses, called farriers. Lots of books were written about how to cure horses' diseases and injuries. People had to look after their horses because they needed them for travelling and farm work.

People tried to keep their dogs healthy too, but only if they were used for hunting. Tudors didn't care much about cats and other animals though!

▲ *Students watching a doctor cut up a body.*

Glossary

amputate cut off a limb.

anaesthetic a medicine used to put a patient to sleep during surgery.

antiseptic a medicine used to clean the skin and make infection less likely.

branded an ancient form of punishment which inflicted a permanent mark on an offender with a hot iron.

dissection cutting a human body open to learn about what's inside.

epidemic widespread outbreak of a disease.

executed put to death for committing a crime.

gladiator a professional fighter in ancient Rome.

gout a disease which causes arthritis, usually in the feet and legs.

healer somebody who cures or treats illnesses and infections.

leprosy a disease which attacks the skin and nerves.

lice tiny insects that can live on humans and cause itching.

operation when a patient has medical treatment that cuts them open to repair something inside their body.

plague a killer infection carried by rat fleas.

smallpox a dangerous disease caused by a virus. it causes scarring of the skin and can be fatal.

witchcraft the use of magical powers.

Answers

Page 4: People in towns were more crowded together so infections spread faster. Country people had fresher food and cleaner water.

Page 6: Good – they could learn basic anatomy. Bad – death by execution wouldn't tell anything about death by disease.

Page 7: It could be dangerous because some treatments might make your teeth fall out!

Page 9: The Church believed that the dead had to be buried whole so that they could live again when the world ended.

A doctor only treating soldiers would not learn about the illnesses of women, children and the elderly.

Page 10: Everyday items were used because the poor could afford them.

Page 11: People might use the wrong herbs, or use the wrong part or wrong quantity.

Page 13: A sharp knife to cut through skin and muscle and a saw to cut through bone.

Page 14: The midwives pictured were probably mothers who would not have as much experience of birth problems as someone working full-time.

Page 18: A royal physician might be punished if he failed to cure the king or queen.

Page 19: It was less risky to keep silent until the queen knew she was actually ill and needed her doctor's help.

Page 20: The paper was hung up until the ink was dry so that it didn't smudge.

Page 21: Poor people could not afford to pay, so doctors made no money out of them.

Page 23: Beggars were branded to warn others what they were.

Page 24: The record shows that 3880 people died from the plague in just one week.

Books to read

Creative History Activity Packs: Tudors
by Jane Bower (David Fulton 2002)

Look Inside a Tudor Medicine Chest
by Brian Moses (Wayland 2007)

The Tudors in Britain
by Robert Hull (Wayland 2007)

Reconstructed: The Tudors
by Liz Gogerly (Wayland 2005)

You Wouldn't Want to be Ill in Tudor Times
by Kathryn Senior and David Antram
(Wayland 2007)

Places to visit

Melton Carnegie Museum,
Thorpe End,
Melton Mowbray,
Leicestershire,
LE13 1RB.
The museum runs workshops on Tudor cures, crime and punishment, fashion, food and drink, and much more.

Websites

**http://www.museumoflondon.org.uk/
English/Learning/Learningonline/features/
viking/viking_2.htm**
Visit this website for more information on the Black Death

http://www.the-tudors.org.uk/tudor-medicine.htm
History, facts and information about Tudor Medicine

http://www.historylearningsite.co.uk/cures_for_the_black_death.htm
Tudor cures for the Black Death

Index